Come Now, My Darling

William M. Hoffman

John Corigliano

I'm lost in this land _____ and fright-ened. _____

To the north is the Vil-lage of Shy

My soul is closed to sweet pleas-ures. _____

Glan - ces. _____

To the east

Rage, bit-ter-ness, ___ and hate ___ con-sume me.

is the Grove of Ten-der Touch-ing. _____

To

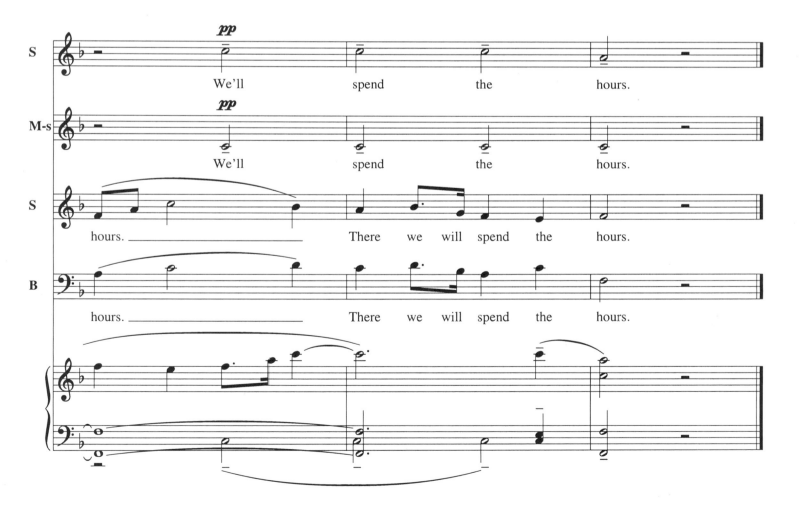

U.S. $8.95

ISBN 0-7935-2520-9

HL50481812

G. SCHIRMER, *Inc.*

DISTRIBUTED BY

HAL•LEONARD®